The 4ᵗʰ of Ju

A Celebration of Independence

The Birth of the United States of America and Her Founding Fathers

By Nickie Summers, Illustrated by Kathy Kerber

This book is dedicated to Steve, Kelsey and
Andy for their patience and love.

Thank you mom and dad for keeping me on the right side of history!!

AuthorHouse™
1663 Liberty Drive
Bloomington, IN 47403
www.authorhouse.com
Phone: 1-800-839-8640

authorHOUSE®

First published by AuthorHouse 9/2/2010

ISBN: 978-1-4520-6635-6 (sc)
Library of Congress Control Number: 2010912011

Printed in the United States of America
This book is printed on acid-free paper.

Republic

Liberty

Happiness

Independence

Life

Equality

Freedom

"Children should be educated and instructed in the principles of freedom."

John Adams, Defense of the Constitution, 1787

Table of Contents

The Story Begins

When we celebrate Independence Day on the 4th of July, we remember the birth of the United States of America and the Founding Fathers. The Founding Fathers were brave men who had the courage to lead people out of the tyranny of a kingdom ruler to create a free country called the United States of America.

The United States of America is a very young country, but her story of freedom and liberty teaches history that is hopeful and inspirational.

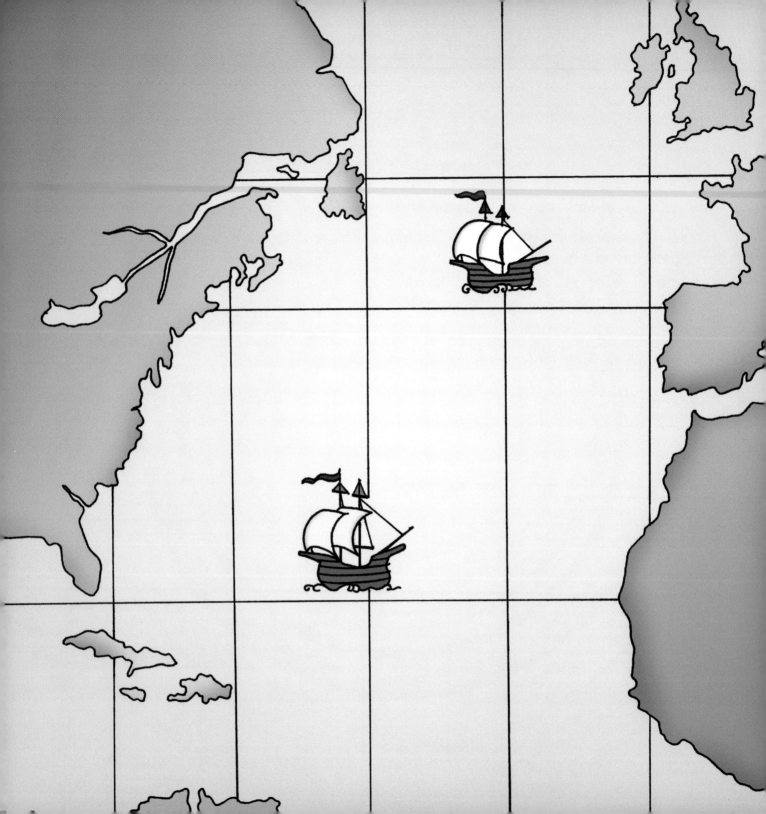

A New World - *The Americas*

On August 3, 1492, a European explorer named Christopher Columbus sailed west to cross the Atlantic Ocean. Three months later he discovered what became known as the New World; it was called the Americas. This discovery was very exciting and news about America travelled all over Europe. People in Europe became curious. Some people set sail across the Atlantic Ocean to see it themselves.

The United Kingdom of Great Britain was one country from where people sailed to explore America. They brought lots of possessions with them from their homeland like tools, clothes, and books. When they arrived, they built colonies where they worked and lived. The people became known as colonists.

The Colonists and King George III –
The Desire for Independence

Over time, the British colonists built thirteen colonies in America and their families grew and grew. They learned skills to earn money, went to school, were devoted to their faith, and became confident in their individual potential. The colonists were hardworking, independent thinkers and grew to be self-reliant.

However, they lived under the rule of King George III who was a tyrant and lived across the Atlantic Ocean far away. To pay for projects in Great Britain, the king often demanded that America's colonists send a large part of their earnings to the kingdom. This demand was made by the king without allowing the colonists to have a say-so in the British government. This made the colonists angry because they were not allowed to participate in their government; this was called taxation without representation.

The colonists became very unhappy and they wanted to break free from the tyranny of King George III. The colonists dreamed of a time when they could live in a free and independent country; a country whose government is responsible to the will of America's people.

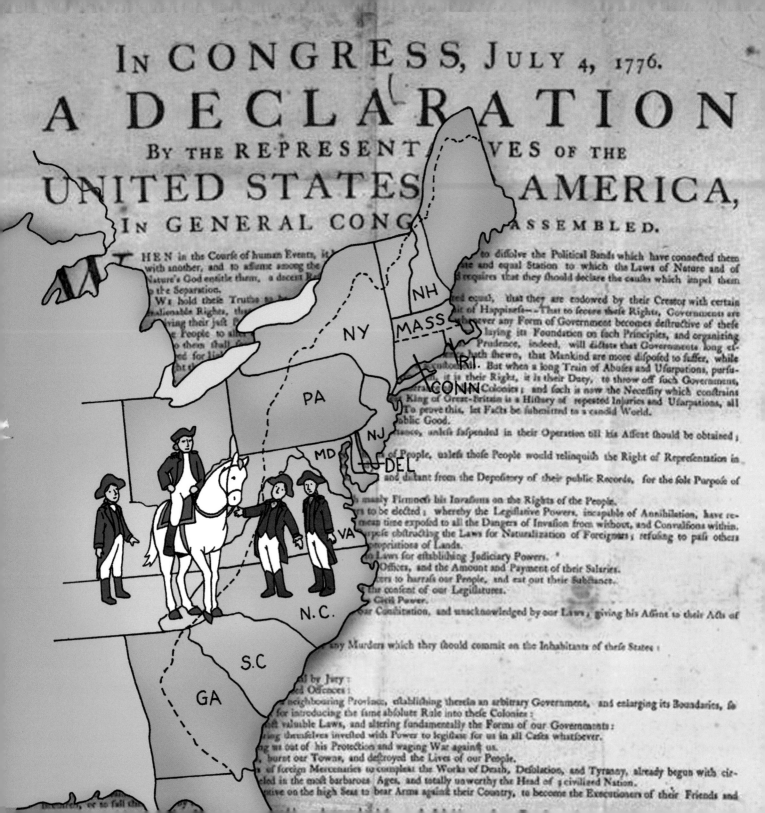

The Birth of a Country – *The United States of America*

Before long, the colonists rejected the authority of the king and the people revolted. This led to the beginning of the American Revolutionary War. It began on April 19, 1775. The purpose was to win independence from the Kingdom of Great Britain for America's people of the thirteen colonies. American soldiers from the colonies and soldiers from Great Britain fought against each other. The master plan for winning independence was led by the Founding Fathers. This was a scary time for the founders and the colonists, but they had great hopes to form a free and independent, self governing country.

During the war, the Founding Fathers gathered in Philadelphia and worked very hard for a long time to create a document that would proclaim America's independence from Great Britain. On July 4, 1776, the Declaration of Independence was revealed. It declared that the thirteen colonies would separate from the Kingdom of Great Britain and the United States of America was born. The colonies now became the thirteen united states of America.

The last big battle of the war ended on October 19, 1781 when British soldiers surrendered to America's army led by Major General George Washington. The war officially ended two years later when the Treaty of Paris was signed by leaders from the United States of America and the Kingdom of Great Britain. This treaty gave the United States of America complete independence and sovereignty as a country.

A Republic – *For the Will of the People*

After independence was won, the Founding Fathers continued to work. It was now time to write the governing laws to protect Americans from ever living under a tyrant again.

On September 17, 1787 the Constitution of the United States of America was complete. The Constitution describes the framework of the federal government and the relationship between the government and America's people. It also explains that members of government work for and are responsible to the will of America's people. This form of government is called a Republic.

Four years later, the Bill of Rights was added to the Constitution to further protect Americans. It explains and sets limits on what the government can and cannot do to peoples' liberties and freedoms.

When writing these lawful documents, the Founding Fathers chose their words carefully. It was their intent to make sure that the reason for creating a Republic would be clear and therefore protected for generations to come.

Washington

Franklin

Adams

The Founding Fathers - *Life, Liberty, and the Pursuit of Happiness*

The Founding Fathers were ordinary people with special talents who worked hard in their communities to build a good life for themselves and their families. They came from different backgrounds and during the founding of the country they served collectively and selflessly fighting for something better, fighting for the future – a free and independent country. Although many people served as Founding Fathers, there are a few that are most notable:

George Washington, farmer and military officer

John Adams, lawyer

Benjamin Franklin, scientist

Thomas Jefferson, farmer and lawyer

James Madison, lawyer

John Jay, lawyer

Alexander Hamilton, financier, lawyer, and military officer

Samuel Adams, merchant

Thomas Paine, writer

John Hancock, merchant

The Founding Fathers were honorable men who had the foresight to know America's greatness. They also inspired new ideas about protecting America's people from an unruly government. They knew that under a small government and a Constitution that demands freedom, the United States of America and its people could prosper.

That's what the founders created when they wrote the Declaration of Independence and the Constitution of the United States of America. They put in writing a very important principle that would forever declare the foundation of freedom and liberty to all Americans. The founders wrote that life, liberty, and equality to all men derive from their Creator, God; not from government. This principle laid the foundation for the spirit of American exceptionalism – *individual liberties that make it possible for every American to pursue happiness to the extent that they want to; not limited to what the government orders them to.*

History teaches that prosperity is best achieved through the lawful, constitutional path laid by the Founding Fathers as written in the founding documents.

The 4th of July – *A Celebration, A Legacy*

In the beginning, the United States of America was often referred to as an experiment. Until July 4, 1776, there wasn't a country on earth that pledged to govern itself by the will of its people. The experiment has lasted for over 200 hundred years and the United States of America has become the greatest country on earth.

This is the story of why we celebrate the 4th of July, Independence Day; the date that marks the birth of the United States of America - *a free and independent country*. It was all possible because the Founding Fathers stood up and fought for principles that laid the foundation of freedom for the American people.

When we celebrate this holiday with patriotic music, summer fun and fireworks, remember the legacy of the Founding Fathers and the lawful document that makes the United States of America a very special country - *The Constitution*.

CPSIA information can be obtained
at www.ICGtesting.com
Printed in the USA
443759LV00002B/15

* 9 7 8 1 4 5 2 0 6 6 3 5 6 *